FABULOUS IN FLIP FLOPS

A Flip Flop guide for the Fashionista

By Robin LeeAnne

My Three Sisters Publishing

Books may be purchased in quantity and/or special sales by contacting the publisher, My Three Sisters Publishing, LLC by email at Publishing@My3Sisters.com or at www.My3Sisters.com.

Published by: My Three Sisters Publishing, LLC

ISBN-13: 978-0615924151
ISBN-10: 0615924158
10 6 1 5 9 2 4 1 5 8

First Edition
Printed in United States of America

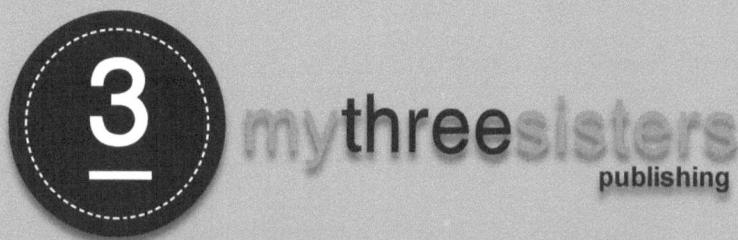

mythreesisters
publishing

FABULOUS IN FLIP FLOPS

A Flip Flop guide for the Fashionista

By Robin LeeAnne

Cover Photo Taken By: Anthony Mongiello

Make-up & Hair Artist: *Kate Johnson Artistry*
www.KateJohnsonArtistry.com
Kate@KateJohnsonArtistry.com

Amazing Photo Above by:
Clarissa Myers Photography
ClarissaMyersPhotography@gmail.com

I want to thank you for purchasing and reading this amazing flip flop fashion book. This book was put together with love, inspiration and my passion for fashion! I want to thank my extraordinary family, friends and fans for their outstanding support. I do truly believe that everything in this world happens for a reason. If you believe you deserve the best, you will GET the best! If you believe you deserve more, you will have more! If you believe you deserve better, you will get it. You have to BELIEVE that you deserve the absolute best to get the absolute best!! Reach for your dreams and achieve everything you want out of life! Enjoy this amazing coffee table book filled with great fashion tips, some marvelous quotes & gorgeous pictures!

Much Love,
Robin LeeAnne
Owner of Francesca's Fancy Flops
Blogger at francescasflops.wordpress.com

Lil' Bella

Learn to live your life with what you've got. Kicking back with my fancy flops.
—Christina Scoleri

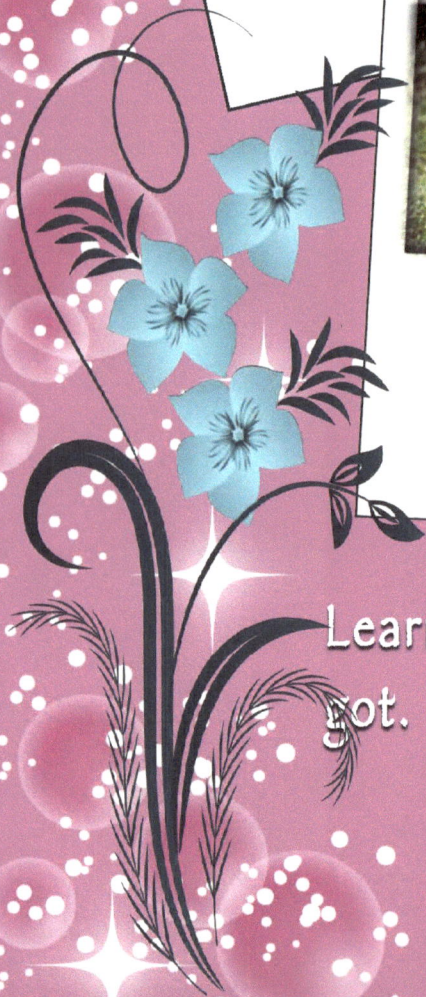

VH 1's Chicago Mob Wives Christina Scoleri flaunting her flip flop love with her adorable dog Bella!

Life is sweeter in flip flops.
—Author Unknown

Wise advice from an acting teacher: 'Always be where your feet are.' Acting happens in the now, moment to moment, your feet can't travel to the past or the future, so stay with them in the present. Then I'd go home and watch my big boxer dogs play, always in the moment, they were the best teachers.

—Patricia Mckenzie
(Actress, Singer, Dancer & Writer)

Photo Credit: TJ Scott

Dear Lord, Let this be a flip flop day.
—Author Unkown

Flip Flop Tip: Polish those toes! Never wear flip-flops without having your toes painted.
—Robin LeeAnne

A Girl Just Can't Live Without: A Pair of Flip Flops, A touch of Fancy & Fabulous Friends.
                    —Author Unkown

Flip Flop Tip: Don't wear your "beach," flip flops with a sundress to brunch. Designate certain pairs for the beach only.
—Robin LeeAnne

Flip Flop Tip: Fancy Flops can be worn from Spring to Fall, even in the colder climates. Flip Flops look adorable with skinny jeans and a loose blouse. Have your blouse make your fancy flip flops. Brown Blouse & Brown fancy flip flops or Pink blouse and pink fancy flip flops. If you don't want your flip flops to stand out or you are looking for a classy look, always match your shirt to your flip flops. If you would like your flip flops to pop, use a bright color. For example, if you have on a black shirt, skinny jeans, throw a pair of hot pink flip flops on to make them pop! Either of these ways makes a great look!

It's officially flip flops season.
—Author Unknown

It's gonna be another flip flop summer.
—Author Unkown

It's never to cold to wear flip flops.
—Author Unknown

A girl should be two things:
classy and fabulous.
—CoCo Chanel

A pair of flip flops is all I need to feel footloose and fancy free. —Elaine Kao.

Elaine Kao is an Asian-American actress of film, television, and theatre. She has appeared in films such as Bridesmaids (the woman from the couple in Kristen Wiig's jewelry store), TV shows such as Entourage (as massage parlor madam Maxie), NCIS: LA (as Xue-Li), Cold Case (as Stacy Lee '09), 24, Eleventh Hour, How I Met Your Mother, The Closer (as An-Li Wong), Curb Your Enthusiasm (as Kevin Nealon's wife, Miyuki), Six Feet Under (as Courtney) & more!

It's always better walking on crystals.
—Robin LeeAnne

Flip Flop Tip: Brides make sure you have comfortable shoes for after your "I DO's," but also make sure they are still gorgeous and have a wedding feel. Don't just throw on a pair of plain white or ivory flip flops. You can also bring in your something "blue," with your flip flops with a blue ribbon or blue shaped heart in rhinestones along the base or strap of your wedding flip flops. Make sure they are something to remember. You should always remember your wedding dress, wedding shoes, wedding jewelry & wedding FLIP FLOPS!

Home is where you park your flip flops.
—Author Unknown

Flip Flops Make Your Toes Feel
like they're on vacation.
—Author Unknown

Gems Between Your Toes.
—Robin LeeAnne

L PHOTOGRAPHIE

Some of the best memories
are made in flip flops.
—Kellie Elmore

Cheerleaders of Murray State University

Photo Credit: Brittany Walls

You walk much sexier in a good pair of shoes.
—Jillian Conley,
Author and TV/Radio Host

Holly is from ABC's Bachelor Pad & ABC's The Bachelor television show (Season 12.) She is also an amazing children's book author.

Flip Flops are the
convertible of shoes.
—Holly Durst Julian

Jennie Raff Photography

Do not let anyone stop you from walking down your path. Set your goals and walk the path you we're set out to walk. Many people will try to discourage you from accomplishing your goals and achieving your dreams. Don't let them. You'll have many people that try to make your path bumpy and difficult, but you keep walking. Hold your head up high & keep on walking in those fancy flops!
—Robin LeeAnne

www.ingramcontent.com/pod-product-compliance
Lightning Source LLC
Chambersburg PA
CBHW060827270326
41931CB00002B/89